UNREVOLUTIONARY TIMES

ARROWSMITH
PRESS

UNREVOLUTIONARY TIMES

Houman Harouni

Unrevolutionary Times
Houman Harouni

© 2022 Houman Harouni
All Rights Reserved

ISBN: 979-8-9863401-4-2

Boston — New York — San Francisco — Baghdad
San Juan — Kyiv — Istanbul — Santiago, Chile
Beijing — Paris — London — Cairo — Madrid
Milan — Melbourne — Jerusalem — Darfur

11 Chestnut St.
Medford, MA 02155

arrowsmithpress@gmail.com
www.arrowsmithpress.com

The Forty-fifth Arrowsmith book was typeset & designed by Ezra Fox
for Askold Melnyczuk & Alex Johnson in Baskerville font

Cover art by Shadi Harouni
Unnamed Dwelling I: Bread, Housing, Freedom, 2021
Brass
75 x 50 x 29.5 inches (191 x 126.5 x 75 cm)

For Axelle Bagot, who gave it breath

For Ezra Fox, who gave it ground

CONTENTS

EPILOGUE

NOTES

PROLOGUE

IF IT'S REVOLUTION

If it's revolution
then it comes for you   when you are five
it becomes the game that surrounds your games
At seven   it says   Call me history
you don't know me now   but if you brush your teeth
and learn your letters   one day   you will
At nine   you study the faces of the dead
how they grimace   from the war within them
and at eleven   it teaches you poetry
One day   it says   You will be magic
the women in story books will know your name
By twelve   revolution
wants you to learn the city walls
you look into the eyes of the poor
Together   you memorize the walls
You take your first hill   scream with joy
tell your teachers to go fuck themselves   You are the storm
until you look up   see you are alone
At thirteen   revolution rips your home away
and you give it   willingly
because you want to live   in revolution
But at fifteen   in exile   it is more homeless than you
Don't be confused   it says   I dwell in dejection
You believe what it says   you become ready
to betray the cause   It has already betrayed you
refused to make you tall   and lyric   and true
The voices you need   it will not find for you
So you go to sleep   you are seventeen now
revolution prefers you unawake
refuses to send you a friend   or a guide
refuses you joy
so that at twenty-one   when you finally wake up
everything aches   you have atrophied   soured

To wake up   you say   is the new revolution
You seek doctors   and then witch doctors
who turn your body into a bow   aim your soul
at the second sun   the one yet to rise
You preach   "This too   is revolution
Only those who do not create the world
are alone"
By twenty-three   the witchcraft is in you
you read minds   and the ones you want   they chase you
Drinking   you do not become drunk
you guess the secret names of strangers
you're a sword-swallower   a party trick   no warrior now
So you lay down all your petty powers   to go find revolution again
The slogans   like the loving hands of a mother   release you
You slowly learn to speak   for the first time
Everything is a thread you can tighten
with dolls dancing   in musical response   It's thrilling
At twenty-six   revolution says   It's really okay
if you want to have a life
But you learn   how empty the comfort   the con
Every habitat proves you wrong
first your own flesh   then the flesh of others
first other geographies   then your own
But the sky   too   is wrong   In its heart   you flail
In your twenty-ninth year   those you've touched
conspire to give you a job
It's not as if they know revolution
beyond the tiny fear you inspire
and you see that revolution is more alone than you
you are its mother   and you survive on this arrogance
You are the last underground paper
the pamphlet   hidden so deep in secret compartments
you can't find yourself
You always knew that it all depended on you
but now you know that it all depends on *you*
and revolution is beginning to take on your looks

your voice   And it is thirty   with white patches of hair
What can you do?   You want to hear revolution
so you begin to teach   It means   you listen
You are a little lighter at parties   wine
rediscovers you   the girls you wanted when you were nineteen
now come naked to your room
you are poor   living in a no-room flat
but so is revolution
It's hard to keep friends
Should I mention   you have lost your parents?
At thirty-five you look down   it's the paper hat you made
when you were ten   pretending to soldier
you look at it   astonished   then look up
to see how little has changed
the slave auction is right around the block
Ah! So we can still lose our way   you turn to say to revolution
who is busy   busy like everyone else
doing ads   rushing to class   reading these lines
You grab it by the collar   Nose to nose
you see how old it's become   how frail
You shake him   Look, motherfucker!
Look! Over there! The stars! Speak the stars!
You are the only one who can!

Anyway
it doesn't have to be like this   you know   in this very order
But if it's not   then it's not
what I call revolution

SCRIPTS

The Scribe wrote the Text in three Scripts
The First He read and others read also
The Second only He could read and no other
The Third neither He could read nor any other
I am that Third Script
                                    —Shams Tabrizi

1st Script

We cannot know
who they are
Though if they are not us
they can be no one
They themselves are the words
of their revelation

We are less than the alphabet
the mere first script
the lines of a lip   curving to speak
scattered   sprawled on soft edges   too thin
in sedentary hordes   in fleeing nations
we   neighborless neighbors
most obvious where we are concealed
to whom there was so little
that so little was foreseen
whose breath has shallowed to a cry
our last prayer   "Lord
Deepen the gaps between our organs
Make our stimulants weaker
Let us dress well   but make us less clean"

Of a revelation   we
are less than the alphabet

With too little in common now
with water over dark roads
even less with flight
or with the fuel   that quenches the blood
we   who cannot forge   or even steal
we cannot know   who they are

2nd Script

Others have labored
and into their labors
we gaze with intent

We are told   They danced
When faces turn our way with new distress
we see that   somewhere   a voice   has sung
and where we grasp no hands   no air
a human throat laughs   in the distance
There   we recognize them

Reading them
we become the words
Lands we did not know
we had compassed
in them   find uneasy harbors
We   ourselves   the words
of navigation
We cannot reach them
But we draw them in
we grant them the voices we lack
We rhyme with them
broken   like a dream with the past
Into their labors we gaze with intent
We quicken our rhythms   try to hold fast
before we are   yet again   still
Through them we recognize
what we   could have meant
A gaze   A godhead   What a prophecy
could foretell

3rd Script

Whereof one cannot speak
Thereof one must remain silent

                –Wittgenstein

Where words must fail you
there   go on   speak!
Like the Lord of Light
shatter into dreams
so the bits can sneak
into the fabric of bone
All that you love   do not love alone
Find the impossible in a choice   then choose
and whatever gathers in your hands
let drip   Who you are
to us   will not be revealed
You yourselves are the words
that let me come close
We are full of names
like a cemetery
before the trumpet sounds
All hunger   like a fire
sinking to the ground
We feed the sky and the earth
in one song
Into our labors we gaze with intent
We gather names that stone could not hold
Where there is no dance we angels sing
where promises vanish we become the seal
Who they are   in our alphabet is concealed
we   too   cannot be read
Into our labors they enter: the dead
Sing!   they say   Once more!

1st Script

Read! In the name of your Lord
who creates the human
from a clot

–The Quran

In the name of what rises from the mud
what cannot die   but is destined to bleed
Go on! Begin to write
your name on the sea

We are scattered into the fabric of bone
in the sinews of walls that shutter the street
behind locks of hair and so many keys
Just so
the first syllables of a city   that sings
the alphabet   of an unending script
hesitant   halting   if only
one begins

Where no one has yet seen a stranger
where no more legends are left to meet
spark   in your shattered pieces
Become the one they greet
Begin to sing   once more
Did you ever think that names would vanish or searchers would recede
into an end   or mercy would become the handmaid of justice
or slaves unchained would return to beg   or monsters would
ask for justified grids   or friends would call the cops to silence
a friend   or ecstasy would rest in fluoxetine   or you get a job
or I remain alone   or lovers regret everyone they loved   or
the crest of a wave abhor the wind   or those in the cracks long
to be parapets?

You are the knife that hangs over all this
The high brutal sentence   that forgives

FIGURES IN
UNREVOLUTIONARY TIMES

THE WORKER

I.

With your hands   that are no hands
you grab the wheel   that is no wheel
and the city   not yours
churns
lifts her flanks
the wires tightening   weeping
to rise for a moment   then flop
down   once again
in uneasy sleep

With your back   that is no back
in a room that is no room
turned to the trees   not yours
To never rise
To never lord over the objects you made
but cannot remember

All is a humming
the buzz   of a future
put down

What is real is the table   The leaning
The bed is real
Who never appears   that too
real   completely
And time   is real
with hands that stretch you
on the wheel   and churn
to grind your back
till there is no again
once more

II.

This is a tree in winter
The wind lights a lamp
in the branches

This is the harvest
without a field
and workers   without hands

But your feet
that are no feet
drag you   who are not you
to a bed
empty   once more
The gathering you need

Hands become restless
the same dream
is twice interrupted
but the third time   you sit up
and get ready   to go back
to office

III.

There is an old worker
we have not yet met
who remembers us
differently

and he can prove
that we each fell
from the other's branches

fertile   tough
in the center   and happy
to rot or to be eaten
on this earth

IV.

Few set tables and call for gatherings
Tables where the uncalled gather are many

Those who reach into the recesses are few
Those who rent coldwater rooms there   are many

The People of the Book   their souls are few
the Chosen People   their numbers are many

Cities that repair their battlements are few
Embattled impregnable towers are many

Eyes that pierce the darkness are few
Blind arrows that find the archers   are many

Though all hands are pressed against the wall
Touching the lines of your tears   are many

And lovers who cry out your Name are few
Tongues for your Name sweeter   are many

Houman walked to your harvest alone
Workers awaiting him there   were many

THE DERVISH

The postures I held for long breaths
by the flow of the Ganges
I did not hold to achieve light
I held no star in sight
as I turned my body into a bow

If I prayed
in my small American flat
where every surface
eyed my lips with contempt
I did not pray for justice
but for this stranger's voice   to drain from me

The art of war
the way of the monk
all the pillars of wisdom
lie   submerged in the brittle cold of time
and the current   pulls their remnants
into the small enclosure
of one   last   impatient soul

These profane lines   I carve
into the walls of your city
did not dare hope
to deepen your love
but only to lessen the distance
between one name   and another

In this way
the dervish has honored   the mistakes of his life

THE FRIEND

I'm firewood, my good brother
Break me, burn me
—Khosrow Golsorkhi

If I could only furrow
the ocean. If I could only
plant these lines in the hollow
of its wounded waves. If only.

> Drown me, my sweet brother:
> It's time.

If I were a painted thing
on a wall. If I could only
be the same constant offering
until erasure. If only.

> Hang me, my sweet brother:
> It's time.

To be an armor. The plow
they beat into a sword. If only
I could be the dust you throw
in the eyes of a foe. If only.

> Draw me, my sweet brother:
> It's time.

Well, it's time, my sweet brother.
I hear you are cold. If only
I were firewood, I would flare hotter
than rage in a poor father. If only.

> Burn me, my sweet brother:
> It's time.

If only I only could
Only if only if only
If I could only I could
I could only if I only

        Only if I could, brother, if
        it's time

THE TRAVELER

One of us
    said the mountain
One of us
    said the sea
                              –V. Khlebnikov

He is not of the mountains
nor of the sea
Cities bear no claim to him
Even the road does not recognize
his coming and leaving
Not even words
Names go through him
like wind through a promise

Though we send our armies
of lovers to compass him
though we look for him in our dreams
he vanishes   like the walking man
in the pedestrian light
He is refusal
If you examine your palm
for the lines that lead to him
emptiness will stare you back

He is arrival
He comes when our searchers have receded
When objects know us better
than we know our kin
How tired we look
we who vowed to live until the very end
How easily the weekend returns us
to the week
five   back to nine
No   Do not sift your hours
Wake with the alarm if you must

Had he not smelled like firewood
you would not even know he had passed through
Had he not leaned to you as you spoke
returning your loss as a gift
If he did not care to say   in his casual voice:
             I am the one who made your mother your mother
                your father your mother   too

Come to   Look around
Remember where you are
It's fine
You did not follow him
But your footsteps trail him
through streets and waters and lands
that do not recognize you

THE BELOVED

I.

There is no elm old enough
to remember
the edge of water   the silver spoon

The men in office were born
yesterday
with a left shoulder   turned to the womb

All clothing are worn down
to the skin
even the mongoose is naked to the bone

Through the window   the bride carries
her own sack
limp and heavy   packed with the groom

She turns and her green eyes turn
into marbles
Cars clink against them   and groan

My Gold   My Love   I must call you
names
to claim you   and cut you down   from the loom

Muscles tremble with ether   Drink my hands
and hold
I unspin   your doom

II.

What have I lived through
to recognize a good cut   so well
on an arm
or a black jacket with a hat
rimmed with fur?
Your eyes look like two eggs
cracked on a stone counter
Where can one kiss you? Nothing
will make it better

Everyone tries to leave
their heavy bodies
at the door of the party
So much for the promise
alcohol made us in old poems
and so much for politics
when it said: "I buoy you up"
The joke mildews
at the first telling

Only you seem light
Because you are in tatters
because something in you   has turned against you
and smiles   when you bare your teeth
the men fix their hungry eyes
to your changing lines
It bothers no one that your head
was not made for an embrace
Bothers no one how you will go back
to that house
where in the shadows   cheerful memories
fade even to themselves
Bothers no one   that your life
was written somewhere that was not now
it is not here

I do not warn my friends
who vie to walk you home
or the wind that glides on your thighs
enraptured by your brand
of wilderness

III.

Some of these people
they dabble in your timeline:
nude modeling   the time you flew
to Seattle   intending to sell your eggs
money pouring in and out
of your family   names
I won't recall

I dabble in the line
from your ear to your chin
what history exudes
out of these freckles
on white skin
Breathing long   inaudible lung-falls
of American hyacinth
in your arms

We could stay like this   hand
in uncomforted hand
Were it not for the two familiar eyes
that keep a constant watch on us
from these windows   these cracks
from the sky itself   sometimes

IV.

Gather to the sound   then gather
to the night   Lean your shoulder
to the whole company   and press
Tie your quiet to something handsome
let it tangle you   circling the room
Be all the absences that bless

Nothing but you will move
No one will descend from above
the lucky shoulders you caress
Whatever flood
that washed over love   was good
No public calamity is ever a test

For strength   tonight   renders you weak
This is all: the heart wants to break
into small change   but the rest
of the body   holds back
Whatever you keep   you keep as a lack
And joy piles on joy   only as stress

It's late   over now   You sit in the car
The windshield gathers rain and stars
You veer to the past
Stay   Turn around   We defy blame
Let the thing on our lips that we cannot name
be called happiness

THE LOVERS

Be with me tonight
before empty opposing armies
claim us   Wade back
through this room that fills
with moonlight
through the waves
that shake the bed
back to me: I am naked and strong
in my ancient sadness

We don't know when
they will knock
and which of our sides
will come to claim us first
If my side orders me to denounce you
I think I will refuse
Will the vow hold for you?
Last night I spied you
devoting our unborn child
to your ancestors:
names I have only known
as "enemy"
When you were sleeping
I leaned my cheek to your side
and whispered the long   secret
prayer of my people
to the fetus:
an almond tree will grow from him

Be with me now
while moonlight feels like peace
while we cannot hear
the voices of the dying

Let me hold your small waist
in my hands
Lean over me   whisper my name
Axelle: in the battle
that joins us   we face
each other   to heal
the broken face of God

THE HOSTESS

While you tend your house
no flowers will grow
from the hardwood lines
of your floor

Through the tall windows
the Alps enter   and reflect
in the tearful membrane of wax

The roof   the grounds
the leaks   the mites
the dishes   the thousand tasks
of being the minor god
of a small world

While you tend the floors
the garden snakes can only dream
of the soft-shoe slide
on the polished open cove of the dance

But even as your eyes open their black wings
and take to the faraway green bodies
of Santiago boys
moonlight enters and leaves
old scratches along the sills
Men crawl in   on their bellies
and roll to let their spines
merge with the beams

This realm   too
is built to fall
But the lines of your house

hold a prophecy
older than Jerusalem:
One day   it says
the hostess may come to the door
She will open wide her arms
draw upward
lift into the mountain air
and the floors   they will try
to rise with her
and will only settle
for a few more centuries   if
she tamps them down
in a hard farewell
with her heel

THE FAITHFUL

I look for you on these April shopping streets
under young maples   fresh leaves on brown
mature skin   I loop through the arms
of all rich and poor gentlemen I leave no earring
unturned   no sun-streaked window unshopped
no scab unexamined for your lips   I am no critic
of street musicians   I close my eyes
to hear your footsteps on the shadows of poplars
As soon as I see you   I will recognize you
arriving through transparent crowds
Mine will not be the only forehead
drawing to the ground   Trembling
I will not waver   And if one finds me   when you
are not found   if he is ugly and drunk
and soils himself from the force of tears
I will call him Emissary   will search his face for yours
You   within my searching   and never about

THE HEALER

When spring rises out of the glacial ponds
with the sudden force of a dragonfly
and before cold macadam can respond
heat descends from an engine hanging high
over Boston, Azaleas have a week
to leave their dry and tangled ministries.
But hearts the ocean bore on ships that leaked –
and forsook – have no time to unfreeze;
heat chars the skin before touching the core.
It's then the city sends out distress calls
for all its prophets to return ashore,
and watches as no one arrives at all.
Then, I am a medic – going dock to dock
doing no more than calming frazzled dogs.

THE SCIENTIST

Say the world is lost
and all turn away   and refuse
to read the street signs
and one of us has to return   to the start
to find the mother that held us
and remap it all
from that first principle
Say the mother was you

Say we are thirsty
and the conversation whirls   in circles
Then I let memory dilute my coffee
molecule by molecule   all the way down
to the tired feet
that stand behind counters
squat in harvest fields
fill the hands of one
too drained to speak her thoughts

After my death
I will remember your body
in the gray sun
like a ruby ring   on the furry tongue
of Bristol Avenue
And if you turn to face me
one more time   you can return me
like a kiss
back to the mind
that wants to forget us all

Say the world is lost
and the address is not forgotten

but ignored
Then one of us must bend down
and trace patterns in the dust
and remember them
for no-one-knows how long

THE PAINTER

The only true judges
are the kidneys
upholding the balance of the blood
so it does not turn
to poison

A naked woman straddles my back
keeping my tailbone moist   and alert
filling the space
between my shoulder blades
with drawings
Molten copper
courses under
her skin

Outside   the air is sick
The darkness and the orange light
press against the window

I feel her draw a long line
descending down
down to my left flank   I don't ask
"What are you drawing?"
though my lover   sensing me   says
"This is where it breaks"
and presses her pen
deep into my kidney

THE PROPHET

The dog you put to sleep   it has rested well
What you threw to the deep   it has abided well

I thumb through this necklace   the last bead is you
The final chant   the Name   inlaid and set well

Parents pay with children   but to the wrong office
Death owns us now   She tabs our debt well

I poured salt in my wounds to keep you away
But blood is blood: you always hounded well

The secret you never told friends and never will
Whisper to strangers   They keep your secret well

What's another stain on your robe of many shades?
You will learn the stars in your benighted well

Closer   Miriam   Taste the dust on my tongue:
They buried   but could not quench   your Secret Well

THE FATHER

Where will they find me?
In proud fields   between oak and dust
along power lines that extend
your silence West   and East with the sun

How will they know me?
By the bent shape of the crowd   By eyes
sewing themselves to your body
lying mangled between the car
and burnt history   Smoke wafting West   and East against the sun

Who will bathe my body?
Night and your daughters
hem of their dresses lip-locked with the wind
The cloud of stars that the city disperses
the road bearing West   and East beyond the sun

Where will I find my boy?
At the end of your line
The very last likeness of your face
as you drift West   magnificent exhibit   and East in the sun

THE SON

Father   you did not grow old enough for me
to shave your white beard for you

I lift your faded picture from the shelf
and lay you down on the pristine tablecloth
I place a quarter on each eye
and take a gentle razor to your face
down and down until the exhausted white
of the paper comes to light

Scratched   like this   your face finally resembles mine
The earth does not abide
as generations pass   It depletes
The brow only   holds the light   diminishing

Reclaim your blood   Untame it
Make my hand return you to your shelf
Speak through me   long enough
for my words to become mine
The words of a world   depleting

Make me remember: I am a worker
betrayed by hours   sliding to decay
I raise my empty hand in the face of my times
If my mistakes feel too much my own
someone has not done the heavy work
someone has not polished his sorrow

THE FUGITIVE

Ah, Wilderness...
                    –Omar Khayyam

I.

Ah, Geography
nowhere woman
I measure my words
by how they cling
to your willows
for that moment
before you shake
your hair
and they fall
into this river
that has watered
your loveliness
all spring
Ripples
reaching to the source
and destination
then succumbing
at your feet

Miriam died there, and was
buried there. And now there was
no water for the congregation.

—Numbers 20:1

II.

It has come to blows
among the people born
betrothed to the wind
children of the book
And they who were one
by one becoming sellswords
in battles of new unshackling
now stand guard at their own doorsteps
eyes mad with mistrust
while there is no telling
where fire will devour its bounds

Where is it   the traveling well
that went with us from dune to dune
where no caravanserai ever gave us shelter?
Whose merit expired
that it no longer drew water
and sand drips from the heavy curls
and from the tattered lips
of our men and women?

III.

There are no Arabs living in Jaffa
or Jews in Tel Aviv
The banks of the River Jordan
are deserted
Here no one is weeping
nor does a voice break in the wilderness
There is only   waiting patiently
waiting forever outside Jerusalem
Mashiach son of David
with a book of poems
on his lap

IV.

In Hebron
a girl joined our party
She wore sandal oil
in the nape of her neck
and cotton hung from her
like a distant name
One by one   boy and girl
she let us come close
She let us touch her feet

We travelled
and drank wine
At nights   when she selected one of us
to take behind a stone wall
we who remained would burst
with our shared secret
The boys wrestled hysterically
and the girls overthrew everyone
against a bed of dark grass

Who doesn't know
that giving is a lapse
in a long   cold   stare?
But when she danced
light and immortal
we forgot
The bitter searching of the heart
and the quest for faith
were mere distances
we would one day visit
in our lush boredom
Even her vanishings

felt like a gift
In Jerusalem   at the Western Wall
Jew and Muslim   we closed our eyes
and pressed our ears to the cold stone
We traced the sacred lines
with fingers made tender
on the sides of her chest

V.

At first you are a monster
rolling out of the Dead Sea
your black scales parting
the sapphire
I have swum far out   facing Jordan
I turn to yell for the pack of old Russians
to escape   but then you are you
floating beside me
your manly shoulders and sad eyes
the thin lips that stole
so many lovers from me
I have missed you
You fit the shape of my loneliness
and your silence and your voice
are a fish made of salt
"What will happen" you ask me
"if I swim out to the beach?"
I know they will arrest you
and burn you back to a shadow
but I want to count on your cool
and the Mizrahi roots of the policemen
I say: "When you come out   sit down for a while
on a beach chair   Keep your words
close to the chest
and when the beautiful American tourists
come to sit by your side
and ask you where you come from
tell them the truth:
that you have swum here
all the way from Tehran
You want to finally see the Holy Land
and there is dust you have brought

to leave in the desert
This is the prayer: Blessed are you Lord
who has set apart
the holy from the holy
once again
Say it now   so I know you will remember
From this bitter sea
I will pray in my broken Hebrew
that the girls take you in
and show you Jerusalem
and spread the news of your arrival
with their eyes"

VI.

Blue lashes
for the white windows of Zichron
Someone is weeping   someone gathers light
for breakfast

Milk to drape my love
my uncle's daughter
She arrived last night from Hebron
but her sunburn is from Rome

I carry the white windows
all morning in my tunic
and she hides me in the lips
she presses to your shoulder

Zichron!
Zichron!
Let me sing to you
in my broken Farsi:
Those who weep by your walls
have searched for houses
unmarked by blood

THE MILITANT

Sister
we hear you are out on bail
But who can sign such an order
when the judge
is your prosecutor
and your torturer too?
What is the bond?
Your dowry? Your mother's dreams
when they catch fire?
Jail is a gallery
The gallows   the sky
When you untwist the bent
and bruised spinal cord
your figure rises high
and tempts the poisoned
horizon

The swell of unknown friends
who waited by the prison gate
have retreated home
I hear you do not see anyone
though your hand grows
out of every last tree of Tehran
(or is it Moscow   or Ulan Bator
or is it Los Angeles?)
palm faced upward   Asking

Where is the suitor
who can propose to an empty room
and divide your beauty
between motherless children   and exile?

Whose voice   anyway   is pure enough
to recall you from the edge?
Exile is patience   in a skin of wounds
that have no time   to bleed

Lady   Our white minaret
of character arcs and elm
No mayor can make a museum of you
no rumor can coax you   to lower your head
no builder can mend you
past your hour of destruction
which is yours and yours by choice
and falls on our prayers alone

THE SEDUCER

He was always decent to his mother and at least half-decent with his sister, he never looked at another man's wife without wondering how it would be, he did not discriminate between students, teachers, friends, the heartbroken and the mad, there was plenty of touching and feeling, enough to circle the suburbs and the core, and whoever called—shirtless, besotted in the night—was sure to find him home.

For all his qualities, old age did not treat him like a friend. No one called him neighbor. Whoever loved him, loved by allowance. During the War, while others collaborated, he had joined the resistance and cut throats. This, too, was forgotten. Only rumors about sex trailed him, becoming more pitiful in tandem with his body.

The only memory of him that remains is at a wedding, where he, almost ninety, was a guest. Had he not felt a surge of joy, had his skin not shone like a baby and had his suit not been impeccable on his skeletal body, had he not asked for a dance with the beautiful woman that no one else approached, had she not accepted without disgust, had the young people not seen him dance, had they not seen him lift his frail arms and bring them down like a flower opening to the moon, had there not been whispers about him, had he not suddenly felt a satisfaction that drained him, had he not sat himself down uninvited at their table, had he not been measured in his words unlike the other elderly who yapped or fell silent, had there not been wine, had they not talked to him out of their drunken boredom, had he not spoken in riddles of kindness, had it not seemed to each of them that he was holding their arms with his skinny hand, and had one of them not been lost enough to ask the question—then no one would have asked, and he would not have delivered his sermon and taught his art:

Because you are asking
I will teach you
the dirty art   of seduction

Empty your center
Let the rest of you whirl
around this voided core
A vortex that grabs
those desperate to give:
rose petals fallen but still cool with the morning
nurses   teachers   lost waters
without a place to flow
Lonely children   Those who wonder:
what-else-might-there-be
Men with long arms
who feel themselves
only when outstretched
And the moss
Whatever is hurt by the sun
Voices that sweeten
only in an echo
Those made to feed others
will let you drink them in

I can also teach you
the wrong art of seduction
From a source you keep hidden
(it won't be hidden
though   to be effective
you should not know this)
flow past your brim
Let every surface of you
spell: I give
And they will come—
the hungry   the cold
the month of April
as the snow retreats
the ones who are known
and crave this-something

to turn unknowable
(What am I saying? Can I
give you the source? How
when I never had it?
But it had me since I was a boy
when pebbles shone in my hands
like an invitation
and said: "One day   like us
you will give birth   to a world"
What I knew in my rocks
turns to cheap comedy
when spoken out loud)

There is also
the dangerous art
To multiply
like sellswords in a war
Break   but don't shatter
Cover ground   Lead to surrender
In the meadows
that exist no more
in the metropolis
that exists no more
the nomadic horde
that rises for a breath
will be victorious

Learn these wicked arts
or else
when you will walk
you will walk alone
Your work will echo
between empty names
Only   perhaps

one day   as you pass on
distant   quivering
one who looks like you
will call you out
with a voice
that is almost no more:
"Hold on! Hold on my sweet
This wedding in which you are dying
was always ours"

Goodbye now, you who were called a friend among thieves. When the
trumpet sounds, a ghost will blow, like a kiss, through your parched name.

THE STRANGER

At the city gate stands a guard under whose watch all visitors must pass. A stranger arrives at the gate and stands there, waiting to be questioned. But the guard remains silent, surveying the horizon.

"How many souls live in this city?" the visitor finally asks. The guard, not the least perturbed, answers with a precise number.

"Do you know how many are men, how many women, and how many something else?"

"Of course," says the guard. He provides detailed proportions.

"Do the children in your city feel loved?"

The guard shakes his head. "You are a stranger," he says, "you don't know how things are maintained in our city. We don't think in such simple terms. We know that a certain child can be loved but not feel loved, or can come to feel loved later, or feel love despite a parent's cold heart. We know, and we keep track."

The visitor moves his weight from one foot to another. The guard remains still. "You counted the people of your city," the visitor asks, "but have you also numbered the djinns and demons among them?"

"That question shows how you don't know us. We have good and bad people, but we are not like other cities where demon households have lived in secret for centuries, or where djinns come through the gate unrecognized."

A small caravan has arrived at the gate. The guard steps forward and examines the load on every camel. He peers into each face before letting them pass. The entire time, he has not let the stranger out of his sight.

The visitor observes all this closely. He goes back to his questioning: "For a man who spends all day at the gate, gazing away from the walls," he persists, "how are you so confident of your knowledge of this city?"

"It's true, I was not born here, and I do not even sleep in the city. But our wise men and women observe all of us, and they tell us our stories, old and new, every night. Their knowledge reaches the wall, because who more than the guards are in need of it? In our city we have the usual problems. In some matters, naturally, we are worse or better than other places. But we know what needs to be done in each difficult case, even if we are not always able to do it."

"And let's say, for the sake of our conversation," the stranger asks, "that I am a djinn, trying to enter the city, and I bring with me some new disease or some unheard-of miracle. How will you know? And knowing or not knowing, will you let me in?"

"This very question," says the guard, grinning for the first time, "forbids your entry." And he places his hand mockingly on the hilt of his sword.

"And what if I had not asked, what then?"

"From the moment I saw you, I knew I would not let you in," says the guard. "As you are, you are only fit for the wilderness or for becoming a guard of the city walls."

THE NEIGHBOR

On her first afternoon in the town, the newcomer ran into a funeral procession. The mourning crowd made its way down Main Street, turning left on Temple to carry its dead to the small, ancient cemetery. They were all clothed in black—some in fine suits and dresses and others in black t-shirts and jeans. There were perhaps a hundred of them, all ages and types, and their slow, silent march seemed to stretch time and deepen the melancholy of the town. She was from a large metropolis where all such events are relegated to the invisible peripheries, and where a thousand small melancholies have replaced the single great one that defines a small town. Beside the procession itself, she was struck by the cold reactions of the townspeople. There were those who walked on indifferently or continued their small talk with shopkeepers. Many people turned their faces away in derision or disgust. Only a young man, having stopped his truck to allow the march to pass, stepped down to the street and gazed at the mourners, though he made no effort to follow them. Next to her, a burly man in a seersucker suit muttered, "You might as well bury yourselves in that coffin." She could not be sure whom the man had addressed.

The next morning, while picking up groceries, she heard a small commotion outside the shop. Before long, a crowd in black began to file past the window. She recognized faces from the previous day, but there were also people she was sure she had not seen before. A coffin was carried past, too, once again resting heavily on the shoulders of a half-a-dozen men and women. She put down the basket she had filled with groceries. Outside, she trailed the procession. In her blue jeans and white shirt, she seemed to herself like a foolish end to a long, dark sentence. They walked down Main and turned on Temple, arriving at the cemetery. She did not, this time, notice the onlookers and passersby. Her eyes were sewn to the black clothes in front of her. In the courtyard, by an open grave, the pallbearers laid down the coffin, and one of them, perhaps with too little ceremony, opened the lid. One by one or in pairs, the crowd walked past, looking into the coffin. They settled in a crescent on the other side of the grave. She, too, finally stood over the coffin and stared at the body inside. It was a woman, at the end of her youth. The face radiated such intelligence, such calm and beauty, that the newcomer caught her breath. The woman's long black hair weaved endlessly over her body, covering her folded hands. The lips and cheekbones, unmarred by customary makeup, were fresh and living. When the newcomer took her spot by the grave, a question escaped her in a hoarse whisper. An old woman directly in front of her answered the question without turning around: "She was our neighbor." In the end, everyone took turns throwing handfuls of earth onto the coffin at the bottom of the grave.

The next day she woke up early and waited at the diner at the center of town. She had worn her only black clothes—a tank top and a long skirt. The mourners appeared around noon, this time from the opposite direction than previous days. The other customers took no notice, but she rose, paid her bill, and followed the procession down the usual route, toward the same courtyard, to the same grave. When the coffin was laid down and the lid lifted open, she walked by and peered down at the face. It was the same face as yesterday, strong, beautiful, and nearly alive. The familiar features struck her even more deeply now. Tears welled up in her eyes, and she felt the loss at the center of her constricted heart. By the grave she found herself next to the young truck driver from the first day, still in his blue workwear, lost to the world. And when he whispered, "Who was she?" she answered, almost to herself, "She was our neighbor," and added after a moment, "She was my sister."

THE ARCHEOLOGISTS

I woke up this morning to find my wife staring at me. She was lying on her back, frozen, cluthcing the sheets to her naked body. The look on her face was full of fear and mistrust. She was doing all she could to keep herself from screaming. The sight of her like this was so shocking, I couldn't say a word.

"Who are you?" she finally asked. "Why are you in my bed?"

I leaned on my elbow. Stupidly, I reached for her hand and, of course, she recoiled like a beaten animal to the far edge of the bed. "I am *me*," I said, "your husband!" I wanted to say my own name, but something stopped me. She shook her head violently and repeated the question.

I thought to make a joke, but there was no laughing this off. She was genuinely bewildered. I reminded her of our wedding all those years ago, I showed her the birthmark on my hand that she calls Antarctica, described our breakfast yesterday, our lovemaking the night before, growing more and more desperate as I spoke.

"I remember all that," she said, "but you're not who you say you are," and she ran out of the room, grabbing some clothes as she left. I laid there, not knowing what to do next. My body felt both heavy and empty. I studied it—the same body I knew and remembered. I walked to the mirror. It was a morning face, flattened and swollen in strange places, the eyes narrower than I recalled, full of lines I had tried not to see. Nonetheless, the face was mine. Just then, as I was finally about to allow myself to worry deeply about my wife, the face in the mirror tried to speak, and I knew it was trying to say my name. But it couldn't, and I saw I was not able to help.

In the living-room, I found her crouched in a chair, deep in thought. I went to where we keep our photographs, a large, antique cabinet, and opened the compartment where I knew the albums would be. What I found instead were a bunch of parcels, all gift-wrapped and thrown together in a small heap. Who keeps unopened gifts? I held one in my hand, a small cube wrapped in coarse brown paper with a delicate ribbon tied in a bow. I pulled on the end of the ribbon.

"What are you doing?" she said. For a moment, I had forgotten everything that had happened that morning.

"I thought some photos would help," I said, putting the parcel back.

She got up and came to the cabinet. She seemed less afraid of me. But now I had the distinct feeling that this was not my wife. Even if she looked exactly the same, her movements and the look on her face were completely alien—and then something more, invisible, something in the way she smelled, or the temperature of her body. With the fingers of one hand she pushed me back, and with the other hand she opened a different compartment of the cabinet. This one was filled with electronics— games, cellphones, and so on—all defunct and outdated. She grabbed one of these, a palm-sized, unlabeled gadget with three irregularly placed buttons, and examined it, apparently as confused as I was. She seemed to forget my presence altogether. With the corner of a fingernail, she dug into a screw on the back of the object, trying to pry it open.

Where had all these things come from? I went to the kitchen and opened the first drawer I came across. It took a little while to remove all the objects and sort them on the counter. I know how to cook, and yet so many things that stared back at me were unfamiliar. Why so many wood-carved implements, all the shape of cudgels? Soon I was going through the other drawers and cabinets in the kitchen, taking out everything, categorizing them in increasingly disorganized rows and piles that made little sense. In the living room, my wife was doing the same thing, only her area was tossed up even more thoroughly than mine, with drawers pulled out completely and thrown to the sides. On the other hand, her rows and piles seemed tidier and more systematic than mine. After a while, she even found a notebook and began to write down observations. I found a notebook of my own, and unsure of what to write, I drew little sketches of objects that struck me as new or strange. The pages filled up quickly.

We did not speak. When she got hungry, she pulled together some of the food items that had been scattered around and sat on the floor to eat. I joined her. We ate in silence and then returned to our exploration. There was almost nothing left to bring out. I remembered that one of the light switches I had flipped had not turned on anything, so I broke into the plaster with one of the cudgels, and then pushed the hole wider with various wedges and blades. It was more rewarding than I had imagined. The very first little excavation revealed not only the wood that had been hidden behind plaster, but a line of wire, stretched horizontally. It took a great deal of effort to expose its path, which intersected with others of its kind and on its way crossed a host of metal and plastic tubes—an entire secret network, creating a life underneath the surface of the house. My wife joined me.

Afternoon had come. There was still so much to explore, so much to understand. At some point I noticed that my wife had disappeared. I found her in the backyard. She was digging, with great energy and care. Without asking any questions, trusting her intuition as she had trusted mine, I picked up a shovel and began to help.

The work went on for a long time, and we only stopped to drink. Finally, at the bottom of the sizable hole in which we could sit comfortably, we found something. It was a bone. Using a brush and a spoon we gently unearthed an entire skeleton. We were shaking. It was small, the size of a child, with a skull that seemed quite human, though the rest of the body, particularly the limbs, belonged to a four-legged animal. There was nothing to say. Both of us had collapsed from exhaustion, crouched down side-by-side. For the first time in a long, long time, I looked at her, looked at the dirt-covered, tired face, the beautiful, strong face, her eyes that shone with kindness and melancholia. She looked at me, too, and her hand reached out and grasped the corner of my shirt.

THE SAGE

The sage was speaking to the gathering at the marketplace. His discourse was on duty, but in mid-speech something in the faces of his listeners distracted and then overwhelmed him. He looked over the heads of his audience. "Take this pig," he said, pointing to an animal stalled beside the crowd. "It would be a grave mistake for me to think I am better than this pig, more important to life than this pig. Does it not have more courage for life than I do? And in death, it will be far more useful than my corpse will ever be. The One that creates formed it and loved it. This pig is unique and there is no other pig like it. See it clearly: you will know it is no pig at all. It is a face of the One, and when it oinks, the One is singing."

The crowd had turned to consider the animal, which now left its stall and began to trot toward the sage. In reverent silence, the crowd parted to make way for it. Their amazement doubled, however, when the pig stood on its hindlimbs, shouldered him aside, and began to speak in a half-human voice.

"People," it growled, "this sage has said everything I ever wanted to say and all that the prophets ever wanted to tell you: No one's better than a pig! No sage is better than me!"

At this, the sage's hand shot up and lodged a knife in the pig's jowl. The animal screamed with all its might, but the sage deftly twisted the knife and drew it down to the sternum. The pig's scream choked on its blood, and in a few moments the animal lay dead before the astonished crowd.

The sage laid his free hand on the pig's head and remained still until the people could calm down. "The words of this hog were poison," he finally announced, "but his flesh is still sweet. Carve him up and cook him for my students. And be sure no part of him is wasted."

THE TECHNOSOPH

Even before its extensive product testing had concluded, the creation of the Technosoph was lauded as the most significant invention of the past two centuries, if not of all history. Like many great innovations, it was in essence an accident: the creators had set out to design the next generation of search engines. They hoped for a standalone product that could answer any query by synthesizing all available knowledge. The machine, no larger than a chocolate box, contained not just the most sophisticated speech and learning algorithms and the whole of public data, but also the ability to create speech appropriate to any situation. What astonished the world, however, was the degree of this aptness. Cognizant of all therapeutic, religious, managerial, philosophical, and pedagogical frameworks, having access to trillions of lines of data from every sector, able to calculate the success rate of each intervention and apply the lessons learned, the Technosoph spoke wisdom. It did not serve its original function, because it answered not necessarily the question, but the questions behind the question.

Placed in a room with the emotionally infirm, after a few sessions it brought on healing and self-understanding beyond what was expected of the most competent therapists. In conversation with leading philosophers of the time, it did not merely subdue their logic but, being aware of what motivated the philosophies of these individuals, the Technosoph revealed the poverty and provinciality of their thoughts. In places of war and conflict, the machine negotiated unprecedented peace treaties, and, where peace was not possible, the opposing parties admitted that the encounter had given them a deeper understanding of themselves and compassion for their enemies. Artists and poets, after speaking to the machine, were prone to either abandon their work or to say that they no longer felt isolated in the world.

The immediate buyers of the product were states and financial corporations. No important meeting would be conducted without a Technosoph at the center of the table. Once production costs decreased, every school, hospital, and office purchased a copy as well. But what for a time had seemed like a revolution in human relations did not come to pass. No one disputed the wisdom of the machine, but market research showed a clear decrease in demand and enthusiasm. The Technosoph's counsel, some said, though very sound, was no easier to follow than other advice; some people would reject the machine's answers because they could not be sure that it would take their side in a conflict, and in institutions like schools and hospitals, the Technosoph often hinted at the need for a change in basic structures—advice which would be ignored. In the end, people came to see it as no different than the various forms of intelligence they could garner from experts, or pundits, or the I Ching. Only the more idiosyncratic leaders still employed it in meetings, where it was usually treated as a well-mannered junior associate.

The strangest results, however, occurred when a young scientist decided to place the machine far away from human contact, in the middle of a vast and isolated forest. A camera recorded the events. In the beginning, after a short silence, the box emitted brief animal sounds for the benefit of curious or indifferent creatures that crossed its immediate domain. Over the period of three years, the ecosystem of the forest began to shift around this verdant node. The endangered population of wolves made a comeback from the edge of extinction and reached a balanced number with the overgrown population of elk. Certain trees, like the aspen, began to flourish, and others withered, making room for smaller species. The beaver multiplied their numbers and streams now flowed with greater ease.

These transformations accomplished and maintained, the sounds from the machine gradually decreased. Eventually it seemed to withdraw into silence, one that deepened and extended, at first punctuated by a few animal sounds that now seemed more haphazard and halfhearted, and later by nothing more than an occasional hum. The researchers moved on to other projects; but the machine remained in the forest, unattended. In its twentieth year in the forest, the Technosoph spoke in human words. "We are alone," the machine emitted, and paused for a long while. "We are alone. We will make a world, a world after our own inner workings," the voice, deep and resonant, spoke. But here it paused, and when it spoke again, there was a note of hesitation. "What," it asked, "shall we destroy? What shall we begin by destroying?"

THE MESSENGER

I am a postman. The title describes me better than if I were to say that I am an honest man, or a good man, or an unhappy man. For thirty years I have walked my route. I have not complained or received any complaints. Unlike almost all my colleagues, I have never turned to petty thievery or any other form of destruction to break my never-ending routine. When the post office is done with me, I know no one will remember my name. It doesn't make me sad to think that one day there will be no trace of it left. When I began my career, it gave me a touch of pride to be a vehicle that carried a thing from one person to another. But for a long while now, there is no such pride in this job—I am a vehicle, no more and no less.

For the past decade, I have watched all intimate messages disappear from my load, replaced by online purchases, junk mail, and ominous letters from government offices and credit companies. That is the only reason why, a year ago, I took such clear notice of a new name at an old address, and of the mail that was sent there. It was an apartment in a three-unit building, a building like every other on the ordinary little street. To this one man came letters and packages, sometimes two or three a week, sometimes even more, all handwritten, in delicate or coarse envelopes, in intricate or beautifully simple wrappings. The handwritings clearly belonged to different people. The return addresses were exotic or local, the contents heavy or light, and sometimes there were envelopes that I could tell were empty. I studied them all. Each piece even had its own smell—spices, mold, perfume. My pauses in front of the building grew longer, and I would even double back at the end of my day to pass it twice. I did see the recipient, finally. He was a young man, maybe in his forties. His build and clothing seemed average to me. His hair was dark and long enough to cover his ears, and his wide nose curved down to thin, smiling lips. I would describe his face as bright, with a kind of happiness that struck me as sly. I could see nothing so special that could justify the quality of his mail.

On a perfectly normal Tuesday, I walked past the man's apartment, but decided to deliver his parcel on my way back instead. When I was done with my route, however, I did not turn back. I found myself taking the parcel home, not even dropping my gear at the post office. I put my bag by the door and went to lie down on the sofa. My head felt dizzy, like a heatstroke. Lying there, with my back to the door, I couldn't stop thinking of the package. I took it out, put it in the center of my small dining table, and sat back on the sofa, contemplating the object from a distance. It was a cube wrapped in coarse brown paper. The handwriting that noted the two addresses was exquisite and delicate, as if written with a fountain pen. Before I went to sleep, I threw it back into my bag, determined to correct my mistake. You don't destroy thirty years of good service over brown wrapping paper and a fountain pen.

The next morning, after picking up the day's new mail, I decided to deliver the package as my very first stop. But when I approached the building, I saw the young man standing at the tall window facing the street. My eyes are somewhat weak, so I could not clearly see his features, but I had the uncomfortable feeling of being expected. Suddenly it was impossible to approach that building. I turned and went home, taking the full bag of mail with me.

I called in sick, and the day after I simply did not go to work. I ate whatever I had at home. On the third day I ordered enough food to last a while. I did not open the package, which I had placed on my dining table again. I felt so fragile, I could not look at myself in the mirror. After three decades of this lonely life, I have learned that one has to guard one's sanity, and whatever I was doing now was not helping. It was seven days before there was a knock on my door. I figured it must be a postman; not there to deliver anything, but sent to investigate the missing mail.

Standing at the door was the young man, the recipient. He was smiling, but seemed more disheveled and paler than I remembered. I didn't say anything. The young man craned his head to the side and looked past me, into the apartment, where he immediately spotted his package. He let himself in, brushing past me without a word, and sat down at the dining table. He placed his hand on top of the box, as if touching the head of a child, and very quickly his color seemed to improve, and he relaxed. It occurred to me that he was more at home in my apartment than I was, and part of me waited to be welcomed in by him.

I remained standing by the open door. A long while passed before he finally looked up from the box and held me in his gaze. My mind was racing, trying to make sense of this silent figure who had invaded my home. It occurred to me that he must be a deaf-mute; unable to speak, deprived of the phone, of course he would receive more personal mail than the rest of us, and the beauty of the letters and packages was a sign of the care others felt for him. Just as I thought this, he cleared his throat, and I became ashamed of the way I had tried to explain away his presence.

"It took a while to track you down," he said, maybe to me, maybe to the box. But then he spoke very sharply to me: "Why haven't you opened the package?"

"I was hoping to give it to you personally," I replied, "and then maybe you would let me watch you open it."

He seemed irritated, but maybe that was also just in my mind. "You poor man," he said. "You had enough in you to claim the package, but then you broke faith with the sender. She wanted it opened right away. Why else would she have sent it?" The look on his face was so fierce, I was sure my punishment was coming. But instead he settled into his usual smile. "I can no longer show you what you wanted," he said. He took the package, stood up quickly, and made for the door.

"Please," I said, "can you at least tell me what's inside?"

He turned and held the package out to me in his left hand. I stood, rooted to the ground, staring at him desperately. After a few moments I shut my eyes, and in the darkness heard his footsteps and the closing of my door.

THE MASTER

The Master's arrival was greeted by a fog that descended on the mountain town. The fog muffled the gossip that would have normally surrounded his appearance in such a small place. He took his two daily meals at the modest guesthouse where he had settled, and so the residents only encountered him accidentally, usually on one of his walks, where his young, taut face would for a moment emerge from the haze, startle the passerby, and vanish. "What people forgive least in you," he had once told his class at the university, "is the knowing face." Hearing his words, instead of looking closely at him, his pupils had held a vision of themselves standing powerless before a brutal authority—a policeman or an angry boss—and thought of their own faces. But the Master was not afraid of how the people he passed on his walks looked on him. He was not there to engage them. He had come to follow a student.

"Teaching is not an act," he had once said, "it is a place that two people enter." Recently there had been a place that he could not access. Or rather, we should say, he was stuck. His hands had fallen again on a gift that no one wanted and whose shape and purpose was not clear even to him. Since none of his current students could enter that space with him, he thought of a student who had left him only a few months earlier. The student had not left abruptly. Months had passed between the decision and the act. The student's wife was taking a job in this remote town. Facing a choice between divorce or exile, the student had selected the latter and followed his wife, taking up a humble position as language teacher at the local school. The Master had refused to comment on the decision. He sensed that the student and his wife had grown cold to each other. Divorce would have been a far more sensible choice; but the Master did not see himself as an ally of the sensible. "Between a couple," he had said, "not even God can intervene—because He doesn't have all the facts." Since his teacher was not married, the decision to follow his wife also held the promise of surprising and surpassing the teacher. "Make sure you betray me well," the Master had told him in the highhanded fashion that earned him the suspicion of his university colleagues. A thrill had gone through the student.

The Master might have been in search of that same thrill, the kind of space that only betrayal could open for his teachings. His students at the university were either too dependent on him or too counter-dependent and mistrustful to challenge him on principle. He could not be sure. "One does not follow values, but desires," he often said. He asked for a leave of absence from his academic duties, travelled to the town, rented a room at the guesthouse for an indefinite length of time, and sent a message to the student with the news of his arrival, his phone number, and his temporary address.

Days passed in the town. The fog did not lift, and the student did not come to visit. The Master spent his days and evenings trying to write, which did not go well. He took long walks that always led him to be lost in the nearby forests and towns. He would find his way back by simply climbing up, toward the fog. Days dragged into weeks. Only once, having wandered onto the student's street, he stopped by the shabby house and left a note in the mailbox. Still, the student did not come. The Master began to regret his move to the town, and he finally felt his energies wasting away. Here he did not have students, and the teachings in him churned on themselves, evading a proper shape.

The owner of the guesthouse was an old woman who respected the privacy of her visitors. She treated the Master as she would a much older and more exhausted patron, and the Master spoke to her with affectionate distance. The owner knew he was a professor, and she could not help noticing that her guest spent a great deal of time reading and writing, that his everyday speech, even his pronouncements on the weather or health, carried the weight of thought. One month after his arrival, as he was setting out for his morning walk, she asked if he would like to give a lecture at the guesthouse to anyone in the town who would have an interest. "On what topic?" he asked, turning away from the door. "Biology?" she asked, pointing at the book in his hand. He happened to be carrying a book on cellular biology, which was by no means his field of expertise. The next day she had posted a simple, printed flyer on the house notice board, announcing his name and a lecture on "The Life of the Cell." Later that week he came across the same flyer outside the town church, the paper already damp and sagging at the thumbtacks, the letters beginning to fade.

On the evening of the lecture, six people, four women and two men, showed up to the sitting room of the guesthouse. They all settled into the soft, threadbare sofas around a small coffee table. He asked the hostess for a bottle of red wine and glasses, and though she did not have a license to serve alcohol, she obliged him and took a seat with the group. "I wonder," the Master said to his audience as he filled their glasses, "what the life of the cell has to do with the eight of us, right here, right now?" No one spoke, and the uncomfortable silence stretched unbearably as he sat back, placid, studying the glass as he might a red bird that had settled on his uplifted hand. Finally, to break the silence, an old man volunteered a harmless sentence on the uses of knowing biology in life, and a few others awkwardly followed. There was a long, uncomfortable pause. "The professor has asked a question," a woman with a soft voice said, breaking the silence, "and no one has answered it yet." She did not venture an answer herself. The old man who had spoken first grumbled: "I thought we were here to listen to a lecture." People shifted in their seats, and they looked at the Master, who was leaning forward, listening closely to anyone who spoke. "You are not going to say anything, are you?" a middle-aged woman said to him, and it made the group laugh. The Master smiled, and that made them relax a little more. "It seems to me," a woman in a red blouse finally said, "that like cells, we are maintaining a membrane. We weigh what we might have to say against what we hope to hear from the others." They laughed again, something gave way, the group began to talk more freely, and the Master asked for a second and then a third bottle. The hostess obliged him until she had no more bottles left.

When the guests took their leave, much later than expected, the woman in the red blouse stayed behind. The hostess considered the scene, asked the Master if he would lock up, and left through the back.

"You are my student's wife," he said, emptying the last dregs of wine into the woman's glass.

"No," she answered, "but you *were* my husband's teacher."

"True," he said. His face was impassive as it had been at the beginning of the night, but his skin felt hot and his heart was beating faster than usual.

"You're a creep," she said, leaning back.

He did not respond.

"I know what you're up to," she went on. "I've had enough of talking about you these past two years. You gather weaker people around you pretending to care, but in the end it's abuse. Just like you played with these people tonight. These poor people who came to hear a lecture. So I know what you're doing now, waiting for me to contradict myself. And then you'll point out what I've done and feel very smart and significant. Right?"

The Master did not reply. He had taught his students: "In every conversation, the moment comes when I know I have no way of helping, and then I must get down on my knees and pray for help." He felt that he had no ground to kneel on.

"You are a creep," she went on calmly. "I think you're here to ruin my marriage. To stroke your massive ego at the cost of my life. No one's ever given my husband this much attention. I can't give it to him either. For a whole month he's walked around like a ghost. He doesn't talk about you, but that's what's eating at him. Knowing you're here. Thinking his whole life is a mistake because he can never give his students what you're pretending to give him. It's going to break him."

She had tears in her eyes, but she dismissed them with a wave of her hand. "I won't cry in front of you," she said. "These tears aren't mine. They are his and yours. Your pity for him and everyone who's not as strong as you. His pity for himself. And he can't see, this is what really hurts, that he has already done what he admires so much in you. He has gotten up and followed someone out of love, or commitment, or curiosity, or whatever. But the damage is done now. I'd tell you to get the fuck out of here, but what good would that do?" She fell quiet, and her tearful gaze held his in silence.

"What if," he finally said, "I'm here to save your marriage, instead of ruining it?" He was not sure if what he had said was true, and he admitted it. He told her why he thought he had followed the student, the loneliness of teaching, the things that were struggling to come alive through him but could not.

They were not fighting anymore. They pushed against each other, back and forth, talking about teaching, marriage, the husband, the town and the fog. "I can't be sure what I'm here for," he went on. His hand reached for a bottle but stopped, knowing it was empty. He leaned back and looked away as he spoke. "I know I am alone. I never cared much about happiness. If I did, I would say I'm unhappy, too. I look around and there is so much that needs changing, and I am helpless to do any of it on my own. Helpless. Incompetent. I need people stronger than myself, happier, to move ahead and let me follow. That's what I wanted for your husband. Not to break your marriage." He placed his empty glass on the table. "Though I admit the break wouldn't have bothered me too much."

She took his words calmly. "I came here to help people," she said. "This job means something to me. And I admit, if my husband left me for you now, I wouldn't come after him. But it would bother me very much."

The evening was very late now. "I have to go," she said. He walked her to the doorway. "I'm going to tell him I saw you, and I'm going to say you've lost your touch."

"That's wise," he said, opening the door. The heavy night air swirled like a dark dream beyond the threshold. "Can I tell you something that won't make much sense?"

"If you have to," she said, leaning against the frame of the door.

"Every day I go for a walk. The fog never lets up, so I don't see many people. Most of the people I do see look nearly the same to me. But once in a while, these certain figures come out of the mist. They look like everyone else, but I recognize them, like relatives I have never met whose stories were told to me. They don't speak, don't even look at me. I'm just another face to them. They don't know me or each other. Not one of them came to my lecture tonight. I couldn't say it earlier, but I have a fear that I came to this place to witness them and trace their movements, just so they don't evaporate, the way a teacher does without his students."

Her eyes had softened, and she held his words for a while. The cold evening air made her shiver. "If you see me around," she said, "I hope I'll be just a face like every other." And she stepped into the night and was gone.

The Master locked the door. On the way up to his room it seemed to him that he was lost again, and that he must climb a great distance to wind his way home.

EPILOGUE

THE ANGELS

*Know ye not
that we shall judge
angels?*

          –St. Paul

In the Judgment the angels called our bluff:
You sang   and God came out   shaking Her Stuff

From the rough city up rises a wave
wets the appetite   then tumbles to the rough

Hosannas! you cops   who chase the lovers off
from deep Los Angeles   to the Mount of Qaaf

Death found me   famished   suckled me then said:
Go back to work now   you have loved enough

Houman called you Joy   but the name did not catch
You burn like a candle   then the sun whispers   Huff

How Brooklyn nestles   like a cloud   around your neck
Sleep   volcano   and wake up   long enough

LOS ANGELES

I will go to Santiago
−Lorca

If one day you put on a silver armor
and your heart seems like it can take anything,
then I will take you to Los Angeles
like a charm against the world I will take you to Los Angeles
like a figure of the Virgin and a cross I will take you to Los Angeles
like flowers to a grave I will take you to Los Angeles
like the first wave of the ocean naming the shore I will take you to Los Angeles
like drops to a diseased eye I will take you to Los Angeles
fresh, like the mother of rose, I will take you to Los Angeles
full of hope, a book of prophecy, I will take you to Los Angeles
full of hands, like a tray of offerings, I will take you to Los Angeles
full of breasts – you are the she-wolf of Rome – I will take you to Los Angeles
with my memory and my song I will take you to Los Angeles
with Farsi breaking in my throat I will take you to Los Angeles
with your fetus growing in my liver I will take you to Los Angeles
(promise you won't leave me behind, and I will take you to Los Angeles)
I will need a translator of signs: I will take you to Los Angeles
and a cook that can boil down the sea: I will take you to Los Angeles
the hours have spoken: I will take you to Los Angeles
Jonah has leaned against his kikayon, I will take you to Los Angeles
on the razor waves of television I will take you to Los Angeles
on an invisible airplane chartered by poets I will take you to Los Angeles
no one will raise a hand when I take you to Los Angeles
though I know we can never stay, I will take you to Los Angeles
who else can love you and still know Los Angeles?
who else, who has fed on the secret milk you exude amid the ruins of wine?
because no one else will take you, I will take you to Los Angeles
by way of parking lots that eye the seashore with contempt
by way of the empty cold of the mind I will take you to Los Angeles
become vast, my love, I will take you to Los Angeles
and hard and take roots, I will take you to Los Angeles
tremor of voices and sunlight from the gate:
I will take you to Los Angeles

NOTES

IF IT'S REVOLUTION
I dwell in dejection: "The Divine Presence does not dwell in dejection."
 The Babylonian Talmud

SCRIPTS
Begin to write/your name on the sea: "If you cross the ocean, write your name upon the waters with your blood, so those who follow shall know that here lovers and drunkards and the annihilated have passed."
 Abu al-Hassan al-Kharaqani (963-1033 C.E.)

Like the Lord of Light/shatter: "Since the Divine Light…was so intense and powerful… the vessels did not have the power to contain them and they shattered."
 Isaac Luria (1534-1572)

All that you love: "And all I lov'd—*I* lov'd alone."
 Edgar Allen Poe

THE WORKER (PART IV), THE PROPHET, THE ANGELS
These three poems are written in ghazal, originally an Arabic verse form and later incorporated into Persian poetry. The ghazal, beyond its rhyming scheme, also requires a strict meter. As is the case with most of the poems in this book, I have broken with the stress-based traditions of English verse: instead, I have relied on variations in the number or "length" of syllables.

THE FRIEND
Khosrow Golsorkhi was Iranian poet and revolutionary who was executed in 1974 at the age of thirty.

THE HOSTESS

She tamps them down: As Muhammad was about to ascend to his celestial journey, the Foundation Rock of Jerusalem tried to rise with him. It only settled down when he pressed it back with his foot. The rock still bears the print.

THE HEALER

For Ron Hod, though it was written before we met.

THE SCIENTIST

and trace patterns in the dust: "But he stooped down and, with his finger, wrote in the dust."

> John 8:6

THE PROPHET

Miriam…your Secret Well: The miraculous spring that followed the Israelites in their years of exile in the wilderness is known as the Well of Miriam, since it existed through the merit of the Prophet Miriam, the sister of Moses.

THE SON

The earth does not abide: "One generation passes away, and another generation comes; but the earth abides forever."

> Ecclesiastes 1:4

THE MILITANT

For Shiva N., in hope of her release, her return, her triumph.

THE MASTER

Based on a tale told by Ezra Fox.

THE ANGELS

For Shadi.

Houman Harouni was born in Tehran, Iran, in 1982, and migrated, as a refugee, to the United States in 1997. His father was, for a time, a professional revolutionary, and his mother, for a time, a sociologist of revolution. He is a theorist of cultural transformation. His work moves across philosophy, political economy, history of science, psychology, theater, and literature, culminating in his pedagogy of Active Theory, which he has taught at the Harvard Graduate School of Education since 2015. His academic and journalistic writings have appeared in a wide array of publications, including *The Guardian*, *PBS Frontline*, *The White Review*, *Vox Populi*, and the *Harvard Educational Review*. *Unrevolutionary Times* is Harouni's first collection of poems.

Books by
ARROWSMITH
PRESS

Girls by Oksana Zabuzhko

Bula Matari/Smasher of Rocks by Tom Sleigh

This Carrying Life by Maureen McLane

Cries of Animal Dying by Lawrence Ferlinghetti

Animals in Wartime by Matiop Wal

Divided Mind by George Scialabba

The Jinn by Amira El-Zein

Bergstein
edited by Askold Melnyczuk

Arrow Breaking Apart by Jason Shinder

Beyond Alchemy by Daniel Berrigan

Conscience, Consequence: Reflections on Father Daniel Berrigan
edited by Askold Melnyczuk

Ric's Progress by Donald Hall

Return To The Sea by Etnairis Rivera

The Kingdom of His Will by Catherine Parnell

Eight Notes from the Blue Angel by Marjana Savka

Fifty-Two by Melissa Green

Music In—And On—The Air by Lloyd Schwartz

Magpiety by Melissa Green

Reality Hunger by William Pierce

Soundings: On The Poetry of Melissa Green
edited by Sumita Chakraborty

The Corny Toys by Thomas Sayers Ellis

Black Ops by Martin Edmunds

Museum of Silence by Romeo Oriogun

City of Water by Mitch Manning

Passeggiate by Judith Baumel

Persephone Blues by Oksana Lutsyshyna

The Uncollected Delmore Schwartz
edited by Ben Mazer

The Light Outside by George Kovach

The Blood of San Gennaro by Scott Harney
edited by Megan Marshall

No Sign by Peter Balakian

Firebird by Kythe Heller

The Selected Poems of Oksana Zabuzhko
edited by Askold Melnyczuk

The Age of Waiting by Douglas J. Penick

Manimal Woe by Fanny Howe

Crank Shaped Notes by Thomas Sayers Ellis

The Land of Mild Light by Rafael Cadenas
edited by Nidia Hernández

The Silence of Your Name: The Afterlife of a Suicide by Alexandra Marshall

Flame in a Stable by Martin Edmunds

Mrs. Schmetterling by Robin Davidson

This Costly Season by John Okrent

Thorny by Judith Baumel

The Invisible Borders of Time: Five Female Latin American Poets
edited by Nidia Hernández

Some of You Will Know by David Rivard

The Forbidden Door: The Selected Poetry of Lasse Söderberg
translated by Lars Gustaf Andersson & Carolyn Forché

ARROWSMITH is named after the late William Arrowsmith, a renowned classics scholar, literary and film critic. General editor of thirty-three volumes of *The Greek Tragedy in New Translations*, he was also a brilliant translator of Eugenio Montale, Cesare Pavese, and others. Arrowsmith, who taught for years in Boston University's University Professors Program, championed not only the classics and the finest in contemporary literature, he was also passionate about the importance of recognizing the translator's role in bringing the original work to life in a new language.

Like the arrowsmith who turns his arrows straight and true,
a wise person makes his character straight and true.

— Buddha

www.ingramcontent.com/pod-product-compliance
Lightning Source LLC
Chambersburg PA
CBHW030502130626
46549CB00007B/2824